Listening With
Your Heart

Listening With Your Heart

COUNSELING THE TERMINALLY ILL

Eula Rae McCown

To order additional copies of this book, contact:
Xlibris Corporation
1-888-795-4274
www.Xlibris.com
Orders@Xlibris.com
36842

DEDICATION

This book is dedicated to Dr. Shannon Cox.

To know Dr. Cox is to love him. He is one of those very special doctors who puts his patients first. He cares about you in that special way that brings comfort and a peace to your soul. He trusts in his God and will pray with his patients when he knows they are comfortable with prayer.

Dr. Cox is one of a kind and anyone who has been fortunate to know him, has received a very special blessing.

We need more doctors like Dr. Shannon Cox.

An Introduction

I am writing this book as the wife of a deceased cancer patient, a caregiver, an ordained minister, a counselor and one who truly listens with their heart.

My journey is not like any others because each of us is a totally different person. I have felt the shock, the pain, the suffering through loss and hopefully, prayerfully, I can ease some of that for you who read this book.

My life has been much enriched by the doctors and theologians I have met along my way. As in any profession, some or better than others. God gave us each a mind and you should choose those that serve your needs as you progress. You know what is best for you to continue your life. Demand the best for you deserve it.

One of the first things my husband said when he was diagnosed with cancer was "God did not cause this. The loving Heavenly Father I worship does not bring this on his children?"

My husband, Mac, had a very painful form of bone cancer. On one of his last days on earth he said, as he said his prayers before going to sleep, "Thank you God, for being so good to me this day." He taught me the body can suffer but the soul can soar at the same time.

What I want to give you, by reading this book, is the peace of God that passes all understanding . . . so peace unto you.

Contents

SOME VERY SPECIAL PEOPLE

The Path I Followed

In 1976, after starting a Meals on Wheels program in the small town in which I was residing, I realized that God wanted me to work with the elderly. In order to prepare myself, I attended North Texas State University, where they had a School for the Studies of Aging. One semester while there I took several courses relating to dying. My husband was shocked at my choice of courses but I explained if I wanted to work with the elderly, I needed to accept dying as a part of living. I could not work with the elderly and when someone died, run from them.

My first two death experiences, as a child, had been terrible and yet I knew I had to expose myself to death to see if I could help or not. The first case, was when my aunt died. Aunt Bell was dad's sister. We had all gathered around the grave and her casket remained open. Just as the attendant went to close the coffin, my fifteen-year old cousin ran yelling and screaming to the coffin and fell into the coffin on top of her mother. This had a terrible impact on my mind . . . I was five years of age at the time.

The second death experience occurred when a neighbor's son drowned. The boy was about eight years of age, one year older than I at the time. He ran away to go swimming with a group of boys, at the swimming hole. He suffered from epileptic seizures, and one occurred while he was swimming in the water. The whole town turned out for the funeral. The service was at our Methodist Church we all attended. My parents took me to the church and the children were separated from their parents and led to the front pews on the right side of the church. I don't know whose idea that was. I can't imagine treating children like that today. The coffin was open and when the service ended, the children were guided to walk by the casket and view the corpse. I will never forget the terrible feeling I had as I saw this childhood friend dead in his casket. A dead person does not look like a living person and it is a terrible shock for a child.

Each one of these experiences occurred before I was ten years of age and I had a terrible fear of death for many years.

I have always been filled with compassion and felt the need to go to people when there is a loss or a problem. I never intrude, but only go to those I know. I have found to be present for them is usually enough. Of course, I embrace them and express my feeling of sorrow and offer to help any way I can. Just for them to know you care enough is a comfort to most.

I have been raised in the church all of my life and have a very strong faith and belief in God. The God I worship is a loving heavenly Father. He loves us with a love we cannot understand. He did not put us here on this earth to play games with us, as a cat does with a mouse. We all have a destiny and He is ever ready to guide, lead and sustain us, if we but ask. I do not believe people understand that God does not intrude in our lives, we have to call upon Him. He is there waiting for us, with his love to help us. We must call on him and this is prayer, just talking to God.

From the day we are born we are dying. Each day we are a day closer to death. I have always feared the unknown, so I decided I'd find out all I could about death and then I would not fear it.

My mother died of the Lou Gehrig disease at an early age. For some unknown reason she feared death up until the last day I saw her alive, in a nursing home, about two weeks before her death. She had been a faithful church member all her life, yet why this terrible fear?

At the time of her first diagnosis, I was working as a church secretary and my office was in the church library. One day a small book caught my attention, "The Christian After Death," was the title. I no longer remember the author, for it has been out of print for many years. I do know the author was a minister. He took each Bible scripture, pertaining to death, and expounded upon it. I read the book believing I could help mama and put her soul to rest. It was hard reading for a thirty-three year old, but by the time I got to the last chapter, I thought how could anyone hold someone back from death when it is the most wonderful thing that can happen to us. Now, I don't think we should all run out, buy a gun and kill ourselves. God put us on this earth for a reason and we are to live our lives to the fullest and then when it comes time to die, be able to know that this wonderful experience will bring us face to face with our loving Master.

The Diagnosis

It was in 1987 that my husband, Mac, was diagnosed with prostate cancer that had metastasized to the bone. Although we had seen his health failing, due to a diagnosis of arthritis, we were not prepared for this sudden shock of the word "CANCER." We found that the word "cancer" seems to change your whole life. It is very hard to live with that diagnosis.

Mac had gone for daily physical therapy, at a local therapy center and this had not helped with the terrible pain he was experiencing. Finally when he got into such severe pain, I phoned the arthritic doctor and told him I had to bring Mac in to see him. He could not continue in such pain. When we arrived at the doctor's office, he took one look at Mac and said, "I'm sending you on to Seton Hospital and we will find out what is wrong with you." When we arrived at the hospital they sent him to the cancer floor and very soon a doctor came in with a pen and a pad, in his hand, and began to ask questions. He said, "We are going to run tests on you and we will know what is wrong with you very shortly." We were both relieved to know we would soon have a diagnosis. We can handle facts . . . it is the unknown that is so hard to deal with.

The next thing we knew they had called in four doctors and all agreed to remove his prostate gland. This is a very hard diagnosis for a man to handle because their sex life is over. I crawled up into the bed with Mac and put my arms around him and told him I loved him whether there was sex in our life or not. We have all known or heard of men who, because of health reasons could not enjoy sex and I had always known I loved Mac enough to live with him with or without sex. Love is love, with or without sex and I did love Mac with my whole heart.

I shall never forget when the surgery was over there were three doctors standing around his bed and Mac asked how long did he have to live. His words were, "I need to know how long I will live so I can bring closure to my life. I have things I need to do." I have since learned that no one knows when death will come except God and we can trust God for He loves us and wants the very best for us. The first doctor replied, "Oh, maybe two weeks." Another doctor said, "We don't know, probably four to five weeks, but that could go on into months." We both decided at that moment that we would just enjoy each day as it came and be thankful for the time we still had to be together. We were very blessed for Mac did live for another two and one half years.

Why are we so busy in our world today that we have to have a life changing experience to help us reach this decision that we should have made much earlier in our lives?

Lord, help us to live each day to the fullest as if it were the last day of our life.

A Religious Experience

It was several weeks before Mac shared the fact with me that he had a religious experience while in Seton Hospital.

The night following his surgery, a nurse entered his room and walked him to a chair where he could sit while she changed his bed. She changed the bed and left him sitting for a while when he said a very bright light entered the room and slowly approached him.

He recognized the light as being Jesus Christ. The light said to him, "You are Mac McCown and because of who you are, this is a part of your life. You are married to Eula Rae and you have three sons."

Mac felt as if he was agreeing with him. Then Christ touched the top of his head and it felt like a warm oil came down and covered his whole body. Then the light left the room.

Mac said a peace and calm came over him and he was never afraid during the whole interaction with Christ. He said it was a very healing experience.

It has been my experience that Christ never comes to frighten but only to comfort.

Remember the doctors had told him he might live for six months and he did live for two and one half years. A lot of this time he had a high quality of life.

Carl Eaton's Story

While attending church at First Cumberland Presbyterian Church in Austin, one Sunday I heard Carl Eaton tell this story. It is one that all should hear.

Carl Eaton was the first pastor of one of the larger Presbyterian churches in Austin Texas. He had been retired for several years when he filled the pulpit at our church one Sunday and told this story.

His wife of many years, Esther, had been diagnosed with a very rare type of cancer. They didn't know very much about it at the time and she was in the hospital. She didn't seem to be in pain, just waiting to die. Carl would go to the hospital and spend the day with Esther and then go home about dark and repeat the same thing the next day.

One day just as Carl arrived Esther was very excited and said, "Carl I wish you had gotten here just a few minutes earlier, for Christ was just here. He was standing at the foot of my bed with his arms outstretched, just like we saw him in all of those Sunday School pictures."

Now Esther had been getting weaker each day and could no longer sit up but she told Carl when she saw Christ she sat bolt upright in bed and put her arms out toward Christ and said, "Yes, Lord, I'm ready to go."

Christ said to her, "No, Esther, it is not time yet, you have one more job to do."

They discussed this, "What was this job Esther had to do?" Carl went home that night and when he returned the next day Esther had just died.

He was so upset with Christ. Christ had not let Esther finish her job.

As Carl related this event to some of his friends they laughed at him and said, "Carl, Esther got the job done. You never believed that Christ appeared to people before, but you know that he did appear to Esther. She got her job done."

Radiation Treatments

Two days following his surgery Mac was to begin his radiation treatments at a large cancer center in Austin, Texas. When I returned to the hospital that morning I had forgotten to bring Mac fresh clothes to wear to the cancer treatment center. He was very upset with me for forgetting the clothes because it meant he would have to go in his pajamas. When the van came that was to transport him to the cancer center, the driver came to his room to pick him up.

He explained to her that I had forgotten his clothes and he would have to go in his pajamas. The driver started laughing and said, "You know as long as you don't try to flash me, we will get along just fine." Then it seemed like everything was just fine. He went for treatments several days and then he was released from the hospital and I started driving him for his treatments each day.

I soon found we cannot live life to the fullest, focusing on death. We are not dead yet and we need to remember that life is good and will go on.

I've always been a person with a very strong faith and I try to live out my faith. But I was not ready for the first trip I made to the cancer treatment center. Mac had already had several treatments. I was determined, if Mac had to go through all of this, I would go beside him right up to the moment of death.

You must remember these are my feelings and not everyone reacts as I do.

I drove to the center and we registered at the receptionist desk. We were soon ushered into an insurance office. Mac was a United States Air Force retired officer and we had excellent health insurance that has always paid off promptly for each bill previously submitted. We were very solemnly told we must pay $500 right then in order to receive our treatments. Mind you, Mac was a retired officer, a retired teacher and a "notch baby" social security recipient. I had just finished going through Seminary to become an ordained minister desiring to work with the elderly. Seminary is very expensive and we really had no "extra monies". We paid the $500 dollars. One does everything possible to try to help their loved one survive this monster "cancer".

We then entered the waiting room and sat for quite some time. No one was talking. Just these austere, saddened faces with this quiet, frightening wait before them, for what? Did these waiting patients know something that we did not? I did not see joy on any of the faces there . . . just silence. When it came time we were asked to follow a nurse through those foreboding doors where only these dying patients went. Then, as we were seated to wait longer, I felt as if we were on a "death march". Were the people here aware of our feelings? I did not think so.

Again we sat for quite some time before Mac's name was called to enter the radiation treatment room. In my heart, I had made up my mind to go with him and stay until the person attending him asked me to leave. As he got up to follow the therapist, my legs would not sustain me and I remained seated. I knew if I stood I would fall and then they would be treating me. All of this time just silence. Yes, we were among the dying.

Mac returned following his treatment. We walked to our car. As soon as I got into the driver's seat I just fell over with my head on the steering wheel and I sobbed like I had never cried before.

I said, "Mac, you are dying and I am too and I may die before you. I don't know if I can survive this or not. Do you know that we were in Hell today?" Now, hell is where God is not and we both knew that and we both felt we had been in hell for the first time in our lives.

Remember these are our reactions, not everyone feels this way.

We made it home and I prayed the next 24 hours as I had never prayed before. As we entered the treatment center the next day, I was amazed at the calm I felt and I talked to everyone I met there. As I began talking to the patients and their families it was as if I put a pin into a balloon. They wanted to talk and tell their stories.

Yes, the radiation therapy turned out to be a miracle in our lives and although we returned often for the long series of treatments, they did extend Mac's life.

We both learned to love the radiation treatment center and all who worked there. This was a loving, healing center and it so completely supported us during our many trips there.

When the treatments would no longer work we were put on Hospice and Mac died at home, with his family, as he had wanted. When he was first diagnosed the doctors had said he might live for a few weeks, maybe that would go into months and now here he had lived for two and one-half years and most of that was some of the best times in our lives. We learned that most important lesson . . . we must live each day as if it were the last and make every moment count. It was then that we had a much better quality of life.

The Hospice Program

While attending North Texas State University in 1980 I noticed they were offering training for Hospice workers. I knew that I had a call from God to work with the elderly and yet at that time I had never been with anyone terminally ill or experiencing death. I was taking several courses, at that time, relating to dying, and my husband felt I was too saturated with dying events, but I felt I must delve into the hospice program. It was quite an experience.

The first evening we met in a large room where approximately 175 people gathered to begin the training. The first evening a quite lengthy film was shown regarding a young mother on the Hospice program. It was a real "tear jerker." This young woman had two children and it took you through her diagnosis and death. When the film was over there was not a dry eye in the room and the next night when I returned for training there was about 10 people returning to study.

When the classes ended I was asked if I would like to work with a hospice patient. I agreed to do so. This was one of the most rewarding things I ever did in my life.

I was assigned a patient, a retired school teacher, living with a niece. The niece was divorced and had two little boys. They had moved the aunt (the cancer patient) into their living room and her hospital bed looked out of a picture window onto a circle of a cul-de-sac. They had birdhouses and bird feeders hanging so she could watch the birds and everything that happened on that street. While the niece was away at her job each day, they hired a nurse who came and stayed with the patient. This nurse was enchanting and the nurse and patient had a very wonderful relationship. I made it a point to go visit with them three or four times each week, even though they lived quite a few miles from my apartment. I even sat with the patient several evenings so the niece and her sons could have some time to themselves.

Of course, a patient is not to have the hospice program until the doctor predicts that the patient has six months or less to live.

One morning I was telephoned quite early and the nurse phoned to say she wished I could come out and see the patient because she had had an unusual experience the night before.

When I arrived they were all excited because the patient had the two little boys visiting in her room, the night before, when she looked up and saw Jesus Christ standing beside a big wingback chair in front of her picture window. When she tried to point Jesus Christ out to the children, they became frightened and ran for their mother. Of course, mother nor children saw Christ, but my friend the patient did. It had the most calming effect on her and she was at peace and ready to go to Christ. She would sink into a coma and then come out and did this several times before she died, within 24 hours of the event. It grieved me that I could not go to her funeral but I was attending school at the time and could not take the time away from my studies.

I became very interested in the Hospice Movement and I was invited to teach on this subject at several Presbyterian Women's retreats at Mo-Ranch at Hunt, Texas during the early 80's.

I felt so blessed by my Hospice experience and when I realized that the radiation was no longer helping Mac we inquired about the Hospice program. He was assigned to Hospice and we were so richly blessed by this program. These workers are trained and they know all of the right things to do for the patient and family.

Several people came to our home to interview us and do a needs assessment. We were blessed by each person that came to our home. First Mac was assigned a practical nurse, which came each day. She bathed him, changed his linens and did anything she could to make him comfortable. Then we had a regular registered nurse and she came once weekly but more often if we needed her and I could always telephone her if I needed her for any reason . . . sometimes just to ask questions.

We had three grown sons and on the Friday before Mac died we had approximately 15 people who came by just to visit, knowing that death was eminent. We insisted on feeding all and felt so blessed by their presence. The two nurses came plus numerous friends.

Trying to Maintain a Normal Life

At the time of Mac's diagnosis we had three grown sons. Our oldest son, Jeff, lived in South Austin about 15 minutes from our home. Our middle son, Steve, lived in Arlington with his wife and their two children and our youngest son, Jimmy, lived in Austin also.

When Mac entered the hospital the first time Steve and his family were planning their first vacation in a couple of years and they were going to go to Colorado. At first they did not want to go but I told them they must go because we had a long stretch before us and I would need him to help me later on.

Our home was a ranch style but you had to go up and down three steps to get in and out of the house. Even to get out of our bedroom we had these three steps to climb and then down into our living room. I realized right away that we must do something to help with the steps. So Jeff and Jimmy cut an opening in the wall of our bedroom leading into the living room. They put in a double folding door. We could close it for privacy, when needed, or leave it open and I could see from my kitchen, through the dining room and living room into the bedroom. I placed a bell beside his bed and he could ring when he needed me. I later purchased a baby monitor and placed it beside his bed so I could go into the back yard and do some gardening, for relaxation, for a short period of time.

Mac was a teacher and always had a book in his hand until the day he died. I knew he needed a hobby to try to keep his mind off of his illness.

He had always wanted to carve wood and had purchased a wood-carving set in England in the '50's. I noticed there was a woodcarving meeting in South Austin on a Saturday so I insisted we go.

When we got there we discovered a new Japanese tool for sale, which allowed you to carve without exerting pressure. Mac showed no interest at all in the tool. We started home in our car and I said, "Mac why didn't you get the Japanese tool?"

He said, "We can't afford it."

I said, "We cannot not afford it." I did a U-turn in the road and we went back and got the carving tool. We also purchased some wood and books of instructions.

Once I got him back into the carving store I had a difficult time getting him to go home. He wanted everything in the store. Our money was limited so I had to tell him he could just spend so much money this one day. When we got home I put a quilt on an old library table in our dining room and then covered the quilt with a sheet. I said, "Let the chips fall where they may . . . we have a good vacuum cleaner."

He had a wonderful time and began carving Santa Clauses which he gave to friends and family.

A few days before he was released from the hospital, Steve called saying he could not stand it any longer, they had cut their vacation short and they were headed home. He said he wanted his children to know their grandfather so they came down most weekends. Sometimes they would come on Friday nights and spend the weekend and sometimes they would just come down for a few hours on Saturday but they did come most weekends.

We had some dear friends from Air Force days that were such a blessing to us. The Walter Warrens would come to visit us about every 2 to 3 months. I like to cook and I would try to fix things they enjoyed. After lunch Warren would say, "OK girls, hit the road." He realized I was house bound and he was trying to give me a break. One Thanksgiving they came and we went to San Antonio to see the Christmas lights. I could not have done this with Mac in a wheelchair but Warren could easily take over and maneuver the wheel chair and he did.

When Hospice took over there were people in our home a lot of the time and they were such a rich blessing to me. I kept a daily calendar with his medications and those days when we would have pain breakthrough and nothing would stop the pain. Finally when I knew the end was near Steve came and moved into our bedroom with us. We had a hospital bed for Mac and two other twin beds. I slept in one of the beds and Steve slept in the other. I would stay up until midnight and then Steve would take over so I could get some rest.

Jeffrey took over the kitchen. He has always liked to cook and he saw that we had food and it was prepared and properly stored. Finally on the last night Jeff insisted that he and Jennie, his wife, spend the night and care for Mac. Steve moved into the guest bedroom and I slept on the couch in the living room, so I could see into the bedroom each time I opened my eyes. Jeff and Jennie were up and wiping Mac with towels all night long.

The next morning I got up and after breakfast took a shower and dressed. Mac could not talk at this time but his eyes would follow me whenever I entered the room. About 9:30a.m. Jeff called for all of us to come into the room. Mac's catheter bag began to fill with blood and he just closed his eyes. His heart had finally quit. Just as this happened, there was a knock at the door and who had arrived but the Rev. Loyce Estes, our dear friend and pastor from the Cumberland Presbyterian Church. We told him Mac had just died and he came into the room, kissed him on the forehead and said a prayer with all of us.

Death can be such a welcome guest. When there is no hope of the patient reviving to lead a normal life, it is time for death. As a Christian we all know our loved ones are with the Lord and we will all be reunited one day in haven.

Moving On

Approximately two months after Mac's death I phoned and made an appointment to visit with the Director of the radiation therapy center where Mac had received his treatments. The day of my appointment I was greeted, for most people there knew me from our previous visits for treatments. I sat down in the Director's office and told her my story as I have shared with you. I told her she needed a Chaplain/Counselor to greet each family to help them through this horrendous ordeal that was facing them. I also shared with her the fact that we had felt "God was not present" at this center, which really shocked her. I must add here that as we became acquainted with the doctors we were often told they were praying for us. I'm sure they did not tell everyone that, but if they knew you prayed, they also prayed.

The Director invited several employees into her office and asked me to again share my story with them. She then told me that there was no money available to hire me at this time. I told her I was not looking for employment, I was just telling her what she needed.

Within two weeks I received a letter from the Director telling me she wanted me to come to work immediately. I had planned a trip and did not go to work until two months later.

There were no directives to guide me through this job, but using my experience, I treated each patient, and their family, as I would have wanted to be treated. Each time we received a new patient I would greet them and tell them I was there to help make this experience better for them. I always asked them, "What can we do here to help make this experience better for you and for your family."

How does one counsel the dying and their family? *From the heart.* When people cry, cry with them. Listen, intently, and try to read into their souls what can be done for them. Sometimes, it is to listen. Touch is also very important at this time.

It is a terrible thing to lose a loved one but when their life diminishes to just pain and suffering, most of us are ready to let them go. Following you will find some stories, about those beautiful people, that gave me a very special gift . . . they taught me that to love, is to live.

Care For The Dying

The following are excerpts from "Care for the Dying," edited by Richard N. Soulen, published by John Knox Press 1976, Atlanta, Ga.

"During the year 1972-1973, an invitation was extended to a group of persons to come together to talk about the meaning of death within the context of Christian theology. Each person was chosen as being representative of a particular discipline, so that together they constituted, in effect, a theological faculty in miniature.

"The following questions were considered by this group: "How do you care for the dying, including yourself? What are the resources of theology as you think about death and attempt to express your care for the dying?" The old pattern of surrounding death and the dying with studied glib avoidance seems increasingly perverse and cruel. Many want to talk about death but have nothing to say, no informed thoughts, no insights or wisdom to share. Even simple concern is cut off by confusion and self-doubt. Indeed, what are we to think of death? How are we to talk to the dying? How can loved ones and friends share feelings and fears? How are we to solve the ethical and moral issues so frequently involved? What practical and intellectual resources are there for the pastor, nurse, lawyer, or the loved one to call upon? In short: How do you express care for the dying?

"This group were to each go their own way and keep account of anything they encountered that dealt with the questions and feelings above and then they would meet again after several months and discuss what had happened to them.

"The first case in this book was a lady going blind who did not want to be a burden to her 76 year old husband and wanted to take her life. The second case was a suicide but a younger man who was insane and did not relate to aging. The third case was an older man who must have heart surgery, was afraid of dying and was plea-bargaining with God. The fourth case was an older woman with leukemia.

"To a large extent, in our society, we have left the individual who is dying alone, because death raises so many problems within us. This book was an attest not only to share the feelings experienced by the person who stands beside the dying, but also those of persons who are in the death process itself.

"Care of the dying goes beyond any professional vocation. It is supra-vocational. Anyone who visits with a person for whom death is an eminent reality may well benefit from exploring the feelings which he has toward his own death and this applies especially to those who work professionally with dying patients.

"Universally as the reality of death is, the process of dying is a highly individualized experience, unique to each of us. We become hardened to death in our society and, culturally speaking, human life is cheap. But when we are faced with this experience personally, our anguish or hope becomes solely our own. It is speaking out of the uniqueness of our own existential attitude toward death that we are at the same time able to reach out and speak to the persons around us.

"A most common death analogy drawn symbolically is that of sleep. A hospital at nighttime presents all sorts of trauma for patients. They have been doing quite well during the daytime with friends and staff, who make up the hustle and bustle of a hospital. But at nighttime many fears come and the experience of sleeping brings with it the fear of possible death. As human beings, we experience the whole range of feelings while in the death process. We may be especially cognizant of the alienation and separation that comes as a result of death. We may be disturbed by the loneliness of the experience and feel the need for someone simply to hold our hand as we died. We may be angry with God for not giving us a chance to finish responsibilities we have assumed. We may simply be afraid that we shall "be no more" after death, and start to wonder why we were born in the first place. But we may also look with anticipation of shedding one's tortured body, of being reunited with deceased loved ones, and of facing God fully and unashamedly can make death an event eagerly sought. When one expects to die in the near future, the moment itself is often not too far away. We are capable of the whole range of emotions. It is an observable phenomenon that we die as we have lived. Our death is not inconsistent with our life, but rather the fulfillment of all our experiences.

"The most important gift to give the dying is to give yourself—honest, open and unafraid. To be with another in the midst of their personal anguish is to offer the gift of humanity.

"In the fourth and fifth cases of dying, the patients, had a feeling of guilt and they were being punished for their guilt. Each stated all they would do for family and God if they could only live their lives over."

"In T.S. Eliot's "Murder in The Cathedral," the archbishop says of martyrs . . .

> "The true martyr is he who has become the instrument
> of God, who has lost his will in the will of God,
> and who no longer desires anything for himself,
> not even the glory of being a martyr."

"This portrait perhaps emphasizes too strongly the individual dimension of faith. However, it does describe the free attitude of one who faces death with a mature sense of meaning. If a person can do this they would be able to face the prospects of their death with freedom and peace. This is also a great help to your loved ones when you die . . . to give this witness.

"The sixth case in the book was a woman dying with cancer. She had been told 25 years before, shortly after she had married, that she would only live for one year and should never have any children. But she had three children, and lived a happy life except for the fact that her husband who was a college English professor had so completely involved himself in his work that she felt they had no marriage. She had contemplated divorce, but she didn't really believe in divorce, she did love him and his children and had a lovely home, just no husband as such. However, she had gotten a job after her children were in school as a counselor and made a full and happy life of service for herself. Now that she was dying her husband had come to her side and they had the most wonderful relationship ever possible between two people and loved each other dearly. He could face her death with her, in love, it was the waiting, year in and year out that he couldn't take and had locked himself into his job. She had such a beautiful Christian attitude about dying and living that she actually did more to help the minister that was to be ministering to her than he helped her. Following are some quotes she told her minister:

> "I know intellectually that this (her death) is the end product of a long process. I've had a long training for this, the acceptance of my own mortality. People try to save themselves. They save themselves for some tomorrow that never comes because unless you invest in human relation-ships, you will never have a life worth a damn. I think we are meant to be spent. We must each decide what we are here for. I feel that we all function at about 15% of our potential most of the time because we are so busy, saving ourselves. What are we saving for? Are we going to use all this up in heaven or is there something better that we can use it for down here?"

"Anyone committed to the task of caring for the dying must be able to hear the multiplicity of their concerns and anguish. The sting of death is not the loss of physical life—that can be a blessing. It is rather the guilt of sin or of a wasted life, which to the dying is irremediable or irretrievable, or it is the loss of all meaning in despair. To care is to discover which of these poses the greatest threat: moral, spiritual, or physical death, and then to speak the word and to become the word in reply. The New Testament addresses itself to all three through its varied interpretations of the meaning of Jesus Christ's death and resurrection: expiation, revelation, and victory over death."

2 Cor 4:16-18

> Therefore, we are not discouraged; rather, although our outer self is wasting away, our inner self is being renewed day by day. For this momentary light affliction is producing for us an eternal weight of glory beyond all comparison, as we look not to what is seen but to what is unseen; for what is seen is transitory, but what is unseen is eternal.

Bernie S. Siegel, M.D.

Dr. Bernie Siegel, a well known surgeon, author was coming to Austin to speak to people who worked with dying patients.

Dr. Siegel had surgery burnout many years ago . . . he had operated on so many people. He would operate on them, only to find them eaten up with cancer. He would sew them up and think they had just a few months to live, yet years later he would see them alive on the street. He decided to change his approach and tried to learn what makes people live when they are not supposed to.

At the time he came to Austin I was working as a chaplain at a radiation treatment center in Austin. I knew the lady who had invited Dr. Siegel to Austin but I could not afford the time to attend his conference. My friend offered to give me a free ticket to hear him speak. I was to go to the ticket booth and give them my name and they would give me a ticket.

When I entered the auditorium, my friend was saving me a seat on the front row beside her.

At the end of his program he informed us that each person has a "life time task" and he was going to lead us to discovering our "life time task." He began by playing music very softly and leading us through a relaxation exercise. Then he told us in order to learn something we needed to go back to our favorite school. My favorite school was Webster High School in Webster, Texas. He then said, "How did you get to school? Did you walk, ride a bus, or your parents drive you?" Get yourself to your school. My home was two blocks down the street from my high school. As I visualized my walk down that shell road, I looked down and saw I was wearing one of my favorite dresses. In those days, sacks that cow feed came in were very beautiful, cotton, print sacks. When daddy bought the cow feed he would try to find several matching sacks and mama would make our dresses from these sacks. The dress was a royal blue, with little yellow flowers and mama had put yellow rick rack around the neck and sleeves. I loved that dress, yet I had not thought of it in 50 years.

Dr. Siegel then told us, "Open the door and enter and go to your favorite classroom." I opened the doors of Webster High School and walked down the hall to my English Classroom. This was also the homeroom for seniors. Inez Bouton was the teacher and a dear family friend. Dr. Siegel said, "Take your seat." I was surprised that I sat in the front seat, third row. Dr. Siegel said, "Now look around you and see everyone you knew." I looked around and recognized everyone in the room, including my high school sweetheart, Mickey Don Moon, who sat right behind me. All of this was so vivid and it was all things once so familiar and now things I had not thought of in years. The most wonderful part is, I was there. Dr. Siegel said, "There is a blank blackboard in front of you. Go to the blackboard and write your life time task on the blackboard." I knew what I was going to write before I started. . . . Use Me God Your Servant . . . .

We were then gently awakened.

The lady, who had invited me to attend the conference, had also brought her pregnant daughter who decided to go into labor. She had to leave to take her daughter to the hospital for the birth of her grandchild. She asked if I would please escort Dr. Siegel back to his hotel. Of course, I was delighted.

On our way to the hotel we had the opportunity to visit for some time. After sharing a death experience of my husband with him, he invited me to come to the closing luncheon the following day. He said, "I will have a place at the head table, some and sit with us."

This is the story I shared with Dr. Siegel: My husband, Mac, died at home with bone cancer . . . it was a very painful death. I kept a daily calendar and he would have pain breakthrough more often as the disease progressed. One day after suffering all day long . . . . About 9 p.m. he said the pain was beginning to subside. He had had nothing to eat all day long but pain pills so I insisted on fixing him a cup of tea and a piece of toast.

We had a prayer ritual that we went through each night but because he had suffered so much that day, I just took his hands and said, "Mac, let us pray." We would pray the Lord's Prayer, The Apostles' Creed, The 23rd Psalm and then each say the things we were thankful for. This night, because he was so sick, I said our prayers alone and then the things I was thankful for and Amen. When I said Amen, Mac said, "No, Eula Rae, not Amen. Thank you Lord for being so good to me this day."

Dr. Siegel said, "This is exactly what I'm trying to teach everyone, the body can suffer but the soul can soar!"

I did attend the luncheon and told Mac's story. The body can suffer but the soul can soar.

Some Very Special People

Case #1

We transported patients into our treatment center, by van, every day and one of the first patients I remember was an elderly rancher from west Texas. He had inherited his ranch from his mother. He was an only child and had never married. He had a wit about him but at first he didn't talk very much. My dad had been a small time rancher, so I was able to talk with him about his stock, acreage, barns, and out buildings, terrain, etc.

One morning, as he arrived in his wheelchair, I greeted him and he said, "You know I've never cried and I woke up several times last night, just sobbing." I told him that I believed he was grieving his death and it was healthful to do that. He said, "You know I don't have long to live, but they don't know that here." When he left, after his treatment, he said to me, "I'm going to see you in heaven." I replied, "I'm going to look forward to seeing you there." He died that night.

Case #2

Dan came for treatments and he was exactly the same age as my husband, same birthday, and he was a retired military man, just like Mac, but he was a retired Colonel. He had lived a very exciting life with a lot of responsibility and now he came in his wheel chair assisted by his wife. His wife was quite small and looked like she had been put through the wringer. He would really harass her, which would in turn embarrass her, bringing her to tears. Often I would take her into my office, just to visit and thank her for being so kind to him. It turned out that one of her main concerns was that after 40+ years of marriage, birth of four children, she believed she was married to an atheist. So, she was concerned about whether he was going to go to heaven or not. She had always been a "church goer" and he just would not go to church or even discuss religion, so how could he go to heaven and be waiting there for her when she died?

These are tough questions and not to be answered lightly. But, I have found with prayer I often, in a round about way, can untie some of these knots people find themselves in.

Finally Dan ended up in the hospital and while he was apart from his wife I thought perhaps I could talk with him privately about his beliefs. Two nights in a row I went to see him in the hospital only to find him sound asleep and a night nurse hired to sit with him. Finally on the third night he was alone and awake. He was very glad to see me and I took his hand and kissed his forehead. We began to visit and he told me he knew he was going to die soon and he was not afraid of death. From my previous experience with Mac, I asked him if he would like for me to message his feet with some of the lotion the hospitals furnish its patients. While massaging his feet, we continued to talk about death. I tried to reassure him by telling him stories people had shared with me. One lady was in an ambulance on her way to the hospital and had been aware her mother, who had been dead for 40 years, accompanied her in the ambulance. It is also known, from those 'near death' experiences, that the dying often see their loved ones who have died before them. So I said, "Won't you have a wonderful reunion with your loved ones who have gone on before you?" He started talking about his dead loved ones and was even laughing about some past stories.

I realized that night that Dan had a very strong relationship with his God and for some reason did not want to share that with his wife. I'm just guessing but maybe it was that 'Top Secret" military officer in him that held back something from her.

I did not get to share Dan's belief in God with his wife until after his death. I did not know he had died until his wife walked into my office one day. Dan had died. She said the day he died he asked her to go next door and tell a neighbor to come over immediately. Seems the neighbor was a 'Bible Thumper' and all of Dan's four children were at home because death was eminent. It took quite a while for the neighbor to get there, for he had to put on a suit first. When he arrived, Bible in hand, the family all gathered around and Dan asked the neighbor to pray. While the neighbor prayed, Dan died.

Then I was able to share with his wife the things Dan had told me when I last visited him in the hospital. These were very comforting to her. She had been busy since his death, for she took his body back to Arlington Cemetery in Washington, D.C. for burial. She was in the process of selling her Austin home and planning to move to Washington to be near her children.

Case #3

I knew when I went to work at this center I would be counseling people with AIDS. Several friends had lost their children to AIDS and one dear friend plied me with many books written re AIDS and the AIDS patient. These books were very hard for me to read but I knew I must, to be more aware of the patients' needs.

One day while sitting in my office I heard the alert call. I did not know what this meant, as I had never heard it before this time, but I knew something was wrong and I stepped out of my office into the hallway. I saw a nurse run with a syringe in hand to a room where the doctor was on the floor with a patient who was having a seizure. They seemed to have everything under control but as I looked around I saw a man with terror written all over his face and I walked up to him and introduced myself. He was the companion of the man suffering from the seizure. I took his hand, sat him down for he looked faint and we visited. I tried to calm him with reassuring words and I know I did because his friend never came for a visit that he did not accompany him and come into my office to visit with me.

It turned out the friend of the AIDS person was a counselor himself. When I was later ordained a Pastor in the Cumberland Presbyterian Church, he came to the service. Turned out he had been raised Presbyterian and he shared with me how much he had enjoyed singing the old familiar hymns he remembered from his church going days. This religious training was still very meaningful to him although he felt so sinful by his life style, he did not want to come to God again. I do think I helped him do that.

One of the biggest problems the homosexual person has is facing their guilt. I believe that people are born with a gene problem and this causes them to be homosexual and they can't help it.

Case #4

One day I recognized a very sick, suffering man and invited him to come into my office. His sister was with him and she also came into the office with him. Jim's parents lived in San Antonio and they had kicked him out of the house when he told them he had AIDS. His beautiful sister brought him into her home to care for him. She was engaged at the time but she and her fiancee had put Jim first before their marriage. She also had a job and had to work his treatment times around her job.

Jim and his sister had the largest, black, beautiful eyes I have ever seen and you could just look deep into their eyes and see their pain and suffering. They were Jewish. After sympathizing with them and telling them I wanted to help them I asked Jim if he had gone to God with his problem. He, in horror said, "No"! I said, "Why not? God, your heavenly Father loves you no matter what. Let's talk to him right now!" We bowed our heads and I prayed for God's love to surround Jim and his sister and for them to feel the loving arms of God surrounding them with His love. When I finished they were crying and hugging each other and I could see the guilt gone from Jim's face.

I saw this couple often and could see such a big difference in their relaxed personalities once they had gone to God, our loving Father in heaven. We became very good friends and when Jim died I received a lovely note from his sister.

Case #5

Another AIDS patient I counseled was David. David was a married man with a small child. David was an angry person. The people working at our center told me he was so rude and angry they did not like to have to deal with him. Each time he arrived at our center, I would go and sit beside him and try to make small talk. He was so ill he reeked evil. Over time I discovered that David's parents lived in Houston. His mother and dad had been encouraged to accompany each other on high school dates and they had fallen in love, but they were first cousins. They married, promising their parents they would never have any children, so they adopted David and his sister. Seems that his sister was an angel and David was just the opposite. He had run away from home, drugged and done everything his parents did not approve of and in using needles he had contacted AIDS. Just by sitting beside him and listening to him each day I learned his wife was abusive to him. By being persistent I had won him over. One day our attendants had just put him into an examining room alone and he asked for me. Again when I went to him I asked him if he had prayed to God. "No! No! Not God". When I did he began crying and it seemed like the anger just melted from him. By being persistent I had won him over. He would have been so easy to walk away from, but inside his body was screaming for help. After days of him talking about the abuse: his wife refused to give him food and even struck him, I got his parents phone number in Houston and telephoned them. I explained to them what was happening to David and told them if this were my son I'd want to know about it. They arrived the next day. Two of the loveliest people I had ever met. The daughter-in-law would not let them into the house and it was only through their persistence of waiting on the porch until David could dress himself and get to them, did they get to David. They stayed in a motel in town for several days trying to get David's wife to do the right thing or let them take David home with them. Dorothy, David's wife, stormed into my office, ranting and raving the next day. I had to close the door and threaten to get our guard to throw her out if she did not quiet down. Of course she was angry because he had AIDS. She had a wonderful job and their young son to raise, living in fear. I nearly lost my job over this case because the wife said I interfered in her husband's case. I did interfere because the patient's life was being threatened by his wife. After about a week it was agreed his parents would take him home with them to care for him until he died.

Case #6

One of the most difficult jobs I had while working with these patients was that of un-cleanliness. One of our patients had the most angelic face and was so dirty the technicians continually begged me to ask her to bathe. Her body odor was so offensive, it nauseated the workers. I decided the best way to handle this was to buy a pretty basket and fill it with pretty soaps and lotions and give it to her as a gift. She still did not use the bath supplies. I finally had to face her face to face. I said, "I'm sure you do not realize there is a terrible odor coming from you." I explained how often when a person's body is chemically unbalanced a bad odor will persist. She said, "I want you to know my husband gives me such loving care. He is a truck driver and his friends trade routes with him so he can always accompany me for treatment. He feeds me, brings me here whenever needed and I just cannot ask him to do more for me." We just had to put up with the bad odor.

She did have grown children and every once in a while she the odor would be less. I just presumed her children would bring her water and soap and help her to bathe.

Case #7

We had a man come for radiation who had cancer of the throat. He was not supposed to be able to speak but he could and was a shock to all who heard him talk. He loved to talk and when he was told he would not be able to talk again it was devastating to him but lo and behold it was not so . . . he could talk and he ranted on all the time. Everyone loved him. He was a jolly fellow and very entertaining.

At the same time he was having his treatments there was a lady receiving treatments and she lived in a nearby town. She would listen to his tales and enjoyed his company. She soon found out he was a rancher and owned his own plane but now would never be able to fly again and had sold his plane.

The last day for George's treatments this new found friend brought pretty decorated cup cakes for everyone in the waiting room to celebrate George's last treatment and she had another surprise for George. Her husband was a pilot instructor and owned several planes. She brought her husband to the party on this day to introduce him to George. Her husband told George he knew how hard it would be to know you could not fly again so he wanted to invite George and his wife to make a date and come fly with him and his wife for the day. He would let George pilot the plane with him sitting beside him. In fact he said, "Whenever you feel like it, just call me and I will take you flying whenever you want to go." There is a lot of beautiful, caring people in this world.

Case #8

Another interesting patient we had was Josephine. Josephine was insane and I thought her to be possessed of the devil. She always insisted on seeing me and then proceeded to rant about her past, which was not very good and she seemed to want to shock me.

One of our nurses came to see me one day and asked me if I did not believe Josephine was devil possessed. I told her, in confidence, I did think this to be true. The next day the nurse brought me a book warning about counseling people like this, for it is thought that if a person is devil possesses the devil can leave the person and go into another body. I had already heard this and I didn't take any chances, for I am a praying person and try to be constantly in prayer with God. I would pray for God's protection before talking to her and afterwards.

Josephine hated her parents. I'm guessing her age to be about 38 and she loved to share wild stories. She had been married four times to different men each time. She was not attractive in anyway and I did not understand how this could have been. I do know the men she had married could not have been desirable people or they would not have married her. I was very relieved when she finished her treatments.

Case #9

Bill came to us with throat cancer and his younger brother was living with him and caring for him. When Bill died, his younger brother, Johnny soon came in with throat cancer. Johnny could no longer live in Bill's rented apartment for his social security check would not pay his bills.

I immediately took him to the local Housing Authority and got him a small apartment in an apartment complex for the elderly. We were most fortunate because this place had an activity center and a free lunch was served daily.

I then telephoned the St. Vincent De Paul Store and was told to make a list of the items we needed and to call before we came in the pickup and we could have all things free. Friends gave a card table, 2 straight chairs a TV set and I went to the St. Vincent De Paul Store and got the rest of the furniture we needed to furnish the apartment.

Johnny was very fortunate that his mother, in her late 80's, lived in a nearby town. She would come and stay with him when he needed her. She was a very beautiful lady, walked and dressed like a queen. At one time she had been the main cook at one of Austin's finest hotels and served in this capacity for many years.

One night Johnny had difficulty breathing and called EMS for assistance. They sent an ambulance immediately. Johnny was black and lived in a black neighborhood. When the ambulance arrived they put him on the stretcher and got him inside the ambulance when a young girl appeared and got into the front seat with the driver. When they arrived at the hospital they whisked Johnny off and asked if anyone was with him and the young girl said she was and they handed her his wallet with all of his money in it. He had just received his social security check and cashed it.

When Johnny was released from the hospital they explained they had given his wallet to his granddaughter. Johnny did not have a granddaughter. I took Johnny to the Police Station and he was assigned a young policewoman to help him. The Center where I worked payed his next month's rent.

One day I took Johnny for food stamps. There had been an error in the amount of stamps he was to receive. We had to wait quite a while to see the person in charge. In the meantime Johnny, who was very ill, kept getting sicker and saying he was not going to make it. Finally I gave him the keys to my car and told him to go start the engine and turn the air conditioner on and wait for me. I had never in my life given anyone my keys to my car before and yet here I had just done that very thing. I just so happened, just as he reached the car I finished the business and arrived at the car right behind him.

Soon after this Johnny ended up in the hospital again and phoned me one morning in a panic. He said, "The doctor is going to operate on me and I will not be able to talk again. Please come help me." I dashed over to the hospital. He gave me the name of the doctor and I in turn phoned a doctor at our center and asked him if he knew the doctor and was he a good doctor. The doctor said yes to all of my questions. After getting the phone number of the attending physician, I phoned his office and asked to speak to him. I told him I was at the hospital with Johnny and I wanted to know why he was going to operate. He said he had explained everything to Johnny but I told him that Johnny did not always understand yet he trusted me when it came to decision making. The doctor then told me what he had told Johnny. The growth in his throat had grown so large, if not operated on it would choke him to death. After I explained this to Johnny he agreed to the surgery. Now, we really did have a big problem for Johnny had just completed the 2nd grade in school and he could not read or write.

I bought Johnny a notepad and pencil and the fun and games began. I would go once a week and buy his groceries and get his medicines. His mother stayed with him most of the time. One night shortly after he had received his social security check a knock came to the door. His mother answered and it was the girl who robbed him at the hospital. Johnny got to the door as fast as he could and locked the door preventing her from entering. She then went to his kitchen window, took a stick and broke the glass pane and tried to unlock the window in order to enter the apartment. I told him I would have cut her hand off with a knife when she put her hand through that window. He managed to telephone the police. They came and arrested her. Seems she was known for stealing people's checks and they sent her back to prison.

Before she was finally apprehended, Johnny disclosed to me his secret hiding place. He had removed the air conditioner grid from the wall and put his money inside for safekeeping. I also bought him a large, wooden baseball bat for protection. He kept it right inside his front door.

I cared for Johnny about six weeks before he died and I found I missed him. Several days a week I would go by his apartment to check on him and try to assist anyway I could. This uneducated, black man was kind, thankful and deserving of a better life.

Case #10

I was delighted to meet a very beautiful young mother one day. Marsha was one of the prettiest ladies I'd ever met. She sat down and told me her life history and I grieved for her. We who come from loving homes do not understand the suffering that goes on in this world.

Marsha looked like she could be a model. It seems that when she was very young she had been given to her grandmother to raise. Her mother lived with the father of a movie star and she was his hostess. He kept her in the most beautiful and expensive shoes and gowns and she did not have time for her little girl.

Marsha's husband was in prison and she did not know of any of the details or she would not share them with me. She was bright, poised and a joy to be around. One day I took her out to lunch at the Hyatt Regency on the lake and she was just overwhelmed for she had never in her life been any place like this.

Marsha lived in a small town and had just opened a gift shop when she became ill. A local doctor examined her and told her "to get ready to die". She was so shocked she drove to Galveston, slept in her "old" car trying to get another diagnosis. The Galveston doctor told her the same thing. She spent 2 nights sleeping in her car not knowing they would have placed her in a hotel if she had only expressed her needs.

Marsha sold her gift shop and there was an elderly person that had a large, two-story home, at the edge of town and left the home to her children. The children put the home up for sale and Marsha bought it. Marsha had two children of her own . . . both boys, one a senior in high school and the other in first grade. She treasured this old house and the time she had there with her two sons.

One day when visiting our patients in the hospital, I saw Marsha's name on the door. I looked in the room but did not recognize Marsha, who was in a coma. Her mother's sister was with her. I motioned for her to come outside. She said Marsha's mother and her two sons were in the waiting room. I met them and prayed with them. Marsha's mother walked outside with me and said she wanted to tell me how much Marsha loved me. The oldest son had just graduated from high school and his grandfather was going to see that he got a college education. He had been an outstanding student. The son would not go unless his grandfather would also take the younger brother. The grandfather did take both children.

Marsha's mother had been kicked out by her boyfriend because she was no longer a beautiful, young lady. He did buy a home for her to live in until she died. She had chosen the town that Marsha lived in but now it was too late. She was quite grieved over the decisions she had made but now it was too late. One can never look back about our decisions, for these days are gone, we can only learn by our past mistakes and move forward.

Each year at Christmas time the Center would select one patient to receive a weeks stay at one of the loveliest hotels in town.

After selecting the patient I would contact the patient to see if they would like a weeks stay at the hotel. We never had a patient refuse. Then I would telephone fourteen of the best restaurants in town and set up two meals a day for their stay at the hotel. The year Marsha was chosen as a recipient she chose to take her cousin and her two boys so the six of them had a suite of rooms. I purchased a large basket and filled it full of games and snacks. We would also buy them Christmas presents. I remember the oldest boy asked for a pair of dress shoes. Marsha's mother told me the boy could not have walked down the aisle for his high school diploma without the shoes we had bought him for Christmas.

Case #11

Lillie was a most interesting person. She was a street person. The few things I knew about her were she had been a cook in Alaska, married at one time and had children living with her mother in Arizona. She was very firm in telling me, "My mother must never know anything about me."

When she first arrived in Austin she had seen a pasture, south of town, with a huge tree in the center of the field and she climbed the fence, took all of her belongings and put them under the tree. When she returned, late in the evening, her belongings were gone.

One of the first things I told her . . . it would be very difficult for me to help her, for I would never be a street person. She asked me how could I be sure of that, and I told her I had a loving family, lots of friends and a church family.

She became ill shortly after arriving in Austin and she was taken to Brackenridge Hospital. They told her she had pneumonia and after a few days released her back to the street. She hitchhiked to San Antonio and ended up in a hospital down there and was diagnosed with breast cancer. She got out of the hospital and hitchhiked back to Austin. This is what she told me.

I advised her to enter an emergency home that took helpless people for 30 days care. She didn't like it because most of the folks there were elderly. She did move in and I promised her I'd help and applied for social security and medicade. When she got her first check she did phone me as I had asked her to. I took her to a downtown bank and she opened an account. I was so afraid that someone would steal her money. I tried to get her into the apartments where Johnny had lived so she could have meals but she did not like them because they had mostly black residents. She then found an efficiency apartment in a seedy part of town. Two weeks later, I was phoned by the manager. She had given my name to call in case of an emergency. Someone had walked by her room that morning and saw her moaning on the floor. They called EMS and they picked her up and took her back to Brackenridge Hospital. She was drunk. Seems she was an alcoholic and just drank until she could drink no more. The second time she did this I went to see the Brackenridge Hospital Social Worker and they placed her in a nursing home. I called and checked on her a time or two and like the time before she was not happy with all the elderly folks around her. It seems that some of the nurses and nursing aides had felt sorry for her. They gave her some nice clothes, and often took her home or on outings with their families.

About five years later I was sitting in a hamburger restaurant on a Saturday with my grandchildren, when much to my surprise the street lady walked by me . . . staggering would be a better word. She was back in her old wretched clothes, battered hat and looking just awful. She paused at my table but I just completely ignored her. Some people you just cannot help.

Case #12

Mrs. Smith came from the hospital, in our van, on a stretcher. She was one of those people you like immediately. She usually had one of her children with her. She had a lot of problems. She had been married, had three sons and her first husband died. Several years later she remarried. Her second husband was a fine man and her sons approved of the marriage but now the husband had Alzheimer's Disease. They were in the process of finding a nursing home for her husband when she was diagnosed with breast cancer.

I do not like to tell negative stories, but we do not live in a perfect world and we have to be able to recognize problems and face them straight on.

She shared the following story with me. Her newly appointed Oncologist had walked into her room about 10p.m. the night before. He proceeded to tell her she was dying and she needed to get her business in order right away. She did not need to hear this at this time. She cried and was still crying when I saw her the next morning. I said, "You have the right to choose your doctors and you can have anyone you want." I even gave her the name of three excellent, caring doctors I knew and she did change doctors the next day.

I was caring for my husband, at home, using the Hospice program when I realized I was running out of morphine tablets on a Friday. I asked the Hospice Nurse if she would telephone this same doctor and get me some more morphine. She said, "Oh! Mrs. McCown, I just can't call him again this day, he has been so mean to me today." I said, "No problem." When I telephoned him he said, "Mrs. McCown, we just need to put your husband into the hospital!" I said, "Wait a minute Doctor, this is my home and I am in charge here. My husband has asked to die at home and he shall. If you won't give me the pills I will call someone else." He said, "Oh, no, I will get you the medication" and he did.

A lot of his patients complained about his poor bedside manner, but you know we do not have to put up with doctors like this.

Mrs. Smith shared another interesting story with me and I did believe her. When her first husband died she was devastated. She had young sons to raise alone. She would sit at her kitchen table long after her children had left for school and cry. She said she could just not pull herself together. One morning while crying at the table, her dead husband appeared to her. She said he was very upset with her and told her she must get her life back together for the sake of their children and then he disappeared. She was so shocked she did not know what to believe. He was dead and yet he had appeared to her, in her kitchen. The next morning he came back again and she said he was so angry with her and fussed at her because he could not enjoy heaven with her acting this way. She said she got right up and got her life back together and in a short time had remarried.

Case #13

Jane confided in me that she was very concerned about her husband. Jane's daughter drove her to the center for her treatments each day. Several weeks prior, her husband trimmed his toenails, and a toe had gotten infected. Jane's husband was a diabetic. The family doctor had put Jane's husband in the hospital hoping to save his foot from the infection. While in the hospital, the family doctor would call in other specialists to check on the husband. These were doctors Jane did not know. One of the doctors had removed a gall bladder unknown to Jane and her daughter. I advised Jane to inform the nurses station, where her husband was in the hospital, that no doctor was to attend to her husband without first talking to her or her daughter. Also, do not let any doctor into his room except his primary care doctor. Jane's husband did survive and so did Jane.

Case #14

This is really the story about two Catholic Priests. They both began treatments on the same week. The first priest was a retired chaplain from the U.S. Marine Corp. He had retired in the East and a lifetime lady friend cared for him but she became ill and had to ask her sister, who lived in Austin to take care of the priest until he died. He would never speak to anyone except when necessary. He appeared to be living in his own world and very irate. His lips were continuously moving and I presumed he was reciting the Rosary.

The other priest came with a big smile on his face and very jubilant. He said, "Guess what? I'm going to meet my master and now I know what is going to kill me!" His hair began to fall out and knowing that I had a huge supply of wigs for all, asked me for a wig. He tried on several before choosing one he could take to his barber and have trimmed. He chose a nice, wavy wig that made him look very handsome. He had as much fun as a kid in a candy store, choosing that wig. It was always a joy to see him come in the door. He was a very loving and vibrant person.

Several years later I was very surprised to see him come into a restaurant in South Austin where I was dining with a group of elderly friends. I went to speak to him as soon as I recognized him, and said, "Father, how nice it is to see you and you look so well." He was as shocked to be alive as I was to see him. He said, "I guess God just doesn't need me yet."

Why ?

I don't know why. But I do know that it is healthy to ask God Why?

At least in your anger and hurt you are not turning your back on Him.

The hardest to understand and accept is the death of a child. I thank God I have not had to go through that horror. But, I do know this. Our Father in Heaven is not happy when our children are born with deformities or have life threatening diseases. When we cry, He cries along with us.

My advice to all is to praise God. This praise can take on many forms. Ask God what is it He wants you to do. Try to be an obedient servant and reach out to others. If we would but treat people the way we want to be treated we would live in a different world.

The only thing that matters in this world is God. And the next most important thing is LOVE.

May God bless you and yours.